FINDING THROUGH WAR

Poems of Fifty Years Ago

© Michael Elliott Binns 1995

ISBN 1 85072 165 3

Printed in Palatino Typeface
by Sessions of York
The Ebor Press
York, England

FINDING THROUGH WAR

Poems of Fifty Years Ago

Michael Elliott Binns

Dedicated to those who fought as I did, but who neither died nor had any ordinary life after the War, and especially to those in the Royal Star and Garter Home.

William Sessions Limited
York, England
for
The Royal Star and Garter Home
Richmond, England

The Royal Star & Garter Home
for disabled ex-service men and women
(Registered Charity No. 210119)

AN INDEPENDENT CHARITY since its inception. The Royal Star & Garter Home began its work in 1916 after Queen Mary expressed concern for the long term future of the many severely disabled young men returning from the battlegrounds of the First World War.

Initially the old Star & Garter Hotel on Richmond Hill was used to house the men, but, whilst this was adequate as a temporary wartime measure, it soon became clear that a purpose built home would be needed in the long term.

The Society of the Women of the Empire raised the funds, and architect Sir Edwin Cooper gave his services as his gift. The new home was opened by King George V and Queen Mary on 10th July 1924 and dedicated as the Women's Memorial of the Great War.

Today the Home cares for some 200 disabled ex-service men and women, offering rehabilitation and respite care as well as a permanent home for those who need it. Some of the residents are war wounded and have lived at the Home for many years. Others have been struck down by disabling illnesses or tragic accidents, and others still are simply here to be cared for in their old age. To all of them the Home is a haven where they can life their lives in peace and security. Therapies, leisure activities, outings and holidays enable every resident to lead as full and active a life as possible.

In this special 50th anniversary year, in which we remember the sacrifices of the wartime generation, the Home is renewing its commitment to the ex-service community it has served for almost 80 years.

This special book, *Finding Through War*, is written by one of that generation and dedicated to the men and women who now live at The Royal Star & Garter Home. By purchasing a copy, you are helping to ensure that the caring can continue and that the Home will always be here for those who need its special care, now and in the future.

May 1995.   Richmond, Surrey, TW10 6RR

                                       Tel: 0181-940-3314

MICHAEL ELLIOTT BINNS was educated at Winchester and St John's College, Cambridge, where he was a classical scholar. He served as a Field Artillery officer in Italy in the war, and was then called to the Bar.

From 1949 to 1976 he served in Church House, Westminster, as Assistant Secretary then Legal Secretary to the Church Assembly, and Assistant Secretary to the General Synod. After 1976 he worked in the London poverty world as Coordinator of Chiswick Family Rescue, the first refuge for women and children fleeing from home because of violence, and then as Funding and Liaison Worker for the Brixton Circle Projects for ex-prisoners and the homeless and rootless. He has continuing interests in the world of prisoners and the deprived.

He married Alison Carey in 1948 and they have a son and two daughters.

Other Publications by Michael Elliott Binns

THE LAYMAN IN CHURCH GOVERNMENT
(Church Information Office) 1956, revised 1964

A GUIDE TO THE PASTORAL MEASURE
(Church Information Office) 1969
'There can be no two opinions about the skill with which this high official has done his difficult job.' *(Church Times)*

THE LAYMAN AND HIS CHURCH
(Church Information Office) 1970, revised 1974
'The highest praise is due to Michael Elliott Binns. The Layman and His Church could hardly be bettered.' *(Church Times)*
'A most readable document on the many sided aspects of the Church of England.' *(The Times)*

NORTH DOWNS CHURCH
A Church and Community History of the Caterham Deanery – 1983.

REALISATION
(Mendip Publishing) 1993
Writings on religious experience and life.

Michael Elliott Binns aged 19 just after being commissioned.

Introduction

IN THIS BOOK *there are 30 poems and 12 short pieces of prose. All were written between 1940 and 1947. It is hard for an author to judge his own work, but I believe that many of the poems in the second and third parts could be published on their own merits. But the justification of the book as a whole is that it is an authentic record of what a boy and young man chose to write at that time, an account of how he found himself through experiencing war.*

I was born in August 1923. It is strange looking back. Through these poems and pieces of prose written 50 years ago I remember.

The book is in three parts, Schoolboy, Soldier, Return. I do not claim that I had a profound insight into the experiences I was undergoing. I do not even claim that an honest account of what I felt at the time is given. But these poems and pieces of prose are what I chose to write. Rather than expressing real feelings they can be evasions of real feeling, because evasion was necessary to enable me to face my life.

I came from an upper middle class background. I was by no means a natural soldier, and had there not been a war I would not have dreamt of becoming one. But that was my fate, and I was expected to become an officer and became one. It was profoundly important to me that I should carry out my duties as best I could, though they might be alien and terrifying.

That is the kind of person I was, and this is what I wrote.

PART I

Schoolboy

I REMEMBER THE FIRST POEM I ever wrote. I was eight years old, and I was still being taught (very capably) at my mother's knee. To my horror I was sent to the dancing class at the nearby town. It was a nightmare experience as I had no idea of how to relate to strange children. But there for the first time I fell in love and wrote a poem to the girl I adored.

> Peggy is the best.
> She does her work with zest.

I was rather proud of getting a word beginning with a z into my poem. I followed it up with poems about everyone in the class, some of them rather rude.

The poem has an importance in two ways. Directly I went outside my home and began to relate I had to write poems. Also my poem was to a girl. It might have been more natural then that I should have chosen to love and look up to another boy, in whose footsteps I might hope to follow. I did not. A few months later I went to my boarding prep school and entered upon a world where women and girls were peripheral, if they were there at all. It is not till the last few poems, written at Cambridge after my return from the war, that I write of the experience of falling in love with a young woman. But then I do.

My prep school was on the whole a miserable experience, probably the worst period of my life. My refuge and consolation was reading, and I found myself writing poetry. I was clever and went on to Winchester, where I was happy. When I had finished my prep I used to write long imaginative poems, bad imitations of Shelly and Keats.

Then one evening my life changed. I slipped in beside another boy in his cubicle and found him with his face transfigured writing poetry. I read what he was writing and resolved from that moment onward to write as he wrote and to follow and love him. We both went on to Cambridge for the year allowed to us, and until I joined the army on my 19th birthday he was the major influence in my life.

There are eight poems in the first part of this book. I wrote others, but they are lost, probably a good thing. The first four that follow this paragraph are Winchester poems, the other four Cambridge poems. Reading poems opens up a world of splendour for a boy, but his own life is narrow. If he also has to write how can he manage? I used my experiences, but had to inflate them so that they became more fantasy than truth. This is true of the second and fourth poems, which are about relating to someone else. I related only to other boys in the dimension of life that made me write poetry. There was attraction, but the idea of homosexual relations never arose. I was deeply moral and would no more consider that than robbing a bank or seducing a girl. The first and third poems are about a life where I felt beauty, but it was lived under the shadow of war.

I

Before a Parting

Sometimes I stop, when, say, I hear
The first creak of a moving gate,
As if my hand sent crumbling down
A barrier between us and fate.

On precipice aswirl with mist
Grimly I strive with Time, and try
To clutch with frantic, hopeless hands
Its windy garments scudding by.

My will heaves high a barrier,
Holds motionless obedient space,
But time uncaring probes for gaps,
And trickles through its massive face.

The seconds' tiny hammer strokes
Still drive the parting wedge between,
And Doom with mind preoccupied
Still trudges on, my woes unseen.

II

A Mountain Scaled

I never loved you till the day I passed
The treacherous surface of your ice-cold eyes,
The glacier torrents frozen from your heart,
The crumbling rocks that lurked behind your smile,
And reached the summit heavy with your frowns,
And saw amid charred homes the druid smoke
Dance its slow dance beneath the hooded clouds,
And in the midst you sat in pride, alone.

But now, made one by darkness, close we stand,
And on the rock's unseen, unfeeling face
We measure out the minutes of our pain,
And hew salvation from its countenance.
Until, eyes blazing unbelief, we gaze
At the first jewels that throb upon our hands.

III

Sometimes the mist of human talk and laughter
Falls away like robes, rolls back and fades in air,
And I am left a pillar, perfectly white and smooth,
Alone on sands, level and shadowless,
Under an even brightness without sun.

But in these outlines, pure and razor-keen,
The phantom steps that dogged me up dark stairs
And through the jostling, crooked streets of life,
Though all the grey-white veils are torn aside,
Still haunt me, heavy in the evening air.

IV

I come to you, not as the tidal sea
Flings straining wave-crests nearer to the moon,
But as the moth, gaze sliding past the stars,
Blunders towards the guttering candle-end.

No greatness ours, but were it so our love
Would be obscurely jostled by the crowd
Of stars that flushed our teeming sky with joy,
No magnet light, mere mark for expert's eye.

But no, it rides alone above our hearts,
Soothing our squalor with transforming hand,
Charming our bowed and withered flowers to bloom,
With skin of moonlight covering stark bones.

My heart wells up with gentleness, sends out
Its delicate arches branching over us,
A fountain blurring the outlines of the hills
With falling films – ambitions, cares, desires.

This is our snow-hut. Here we snuggle deep
In fur of darkness, kindled with our hearts,
The world shrunk to our pin-point hemisphere,
Swollen our snow-hut to the curve of sky.

And Time, the background whisperer, does not dare
The blizzard's fierce, deliberate wall of steel,
Or else lies frozen, buried half in snow
And half in darkness – will not worry us.

Here is our refuge, bars out memory,
The traveller with his bag of petty fears,
Smothers the ice-bound world's imperious knock.
Cloud shadows fumble on its walls in vain.

Forget the star-graspers, they who set alight
Their generation's beacon, they who were
Fuel for the trail that reddens down our night –
Forget, for we are kings, because alone.

This is our journey's end, and here we grasp,
Life's topmost peak, forgetfulness of life.
Here is our pole, and here our place of rest.
The North Star holds the centre of our sky.

The next four poems are Cambridge poems. Cambridge at this time was a transitional place, meaning little compared to Winchester. Two aspects of my life there were important. One was my continuing relationship with my Winchester friend, and the fifth poem expresses this with a depth of feeling wholly different from the two poems of affection written earlier. The other aspect was my training for war. Because of a chance encounter I joined the Field Artillery Officers Training Unit, not the Infantry. It was expected of me that I should become an officer. I don't think I could have been an effective infantry officer, but I was an effective gunner officer, though by no means a conventional one. The last poem is short and simple. After an exercise we were boarding our vehicles for a long drive back to Cambridge. I was hesitating and an older undergraduate, who was a lance bombardier, called me up beside him. I found that this act of kindness drew me to love him, and I think he realised it and felt love towards me.

The sixth poem is about my Devonshire village, where I lived from just before the beginning of the war until I joined up. It was the first home where I wanted to be and was part of the wider community beyond the walls of my house. But it was quite a different community to that of school and university. This led to a tension in me. To which of the two should I belong? The seventh poem in an oblique way expresses this tension.

V

Before you came my world was ice,
A Buddha's hunched and hopeless form.
A North Pole scarcely moving in
The universal whirling storm.

Along the grey horizon boughs
Shed leaves of calendars like tears,
Drifting aloof as snow to swell
The chaos of the withering years.

You stood beneath the trees and caught
The moments as they fell to earth.
Beneath your touch they flowered out
In positive and lasting worth.

Ours have been sky-lark singing hours
Above the clouds' heat-swooning glade,
But far below grief's shrill monsoon
Beats on a wilderness of shade

No life is this. Only across
The storm a lovely lightning flash.
We feel far off the tug of earth,
The summons of imperious flesh.

Now we must go. You would not stay.
Life beckons with its blaze of years.
Each crevice blooms with flowers for you,
Down alleys with blind walls of tears.

But I must mint my currency
From transient and golden days
To pay my bitter passage through
The mud-flats left by ebbing joys.

And may your spirit be to me
As the firm comfort of the North,
Whose grip gropes over darkened seas
To clamp me on my wished for course.

Or will a stranger with cold eyes
Blow on the ashes of his heart,
Scrabble with clawing hands to rend
The unmoved mountain face apart?

The sixth and visionary sense
Is gone, the magic Sesame.
The granite warder grimly waits
To take the only entrance fee.

One mansion of my heart has lost
Its owner's quickening touch, may die,
Withdraw into itself, grow strange,
A blank facade, a sightless eye.

Behind the shutters gradually
The dust collect on memories,
And hover about the darkened rooms,
That counterfeit the underseas.

VI

The evening world moves softly, afraid to spill
The dreaming waters of air's still lagoon,
Or ruffle its calm surface, and the sun
Like sea-birds skims the corn-brown sweep of hill.

This is a time of contact, this an hour
Poised and important, while renewal creeps
Along triumphant veins, and finger-tips
Touch softly, tingling with electric power.

A page is turned.   Never the same again.
Dawn's ripple widens in the pool of night,
Leading the eye down galleries of light,
My pit-shafts probing in the deep unknown.

This has not spot-light's splendour and surprise
To bring at one stride through the walls of night
A sudden edifice of towering thought,
Massive and jewel-perfect to the eyes.

Rather tall wave that inches further creeps,
Advancing across the sand the stain of dark
Towards the mysterious high-water-mark,
The terminus where lines converging meet.

And will return, when mind like sunlight rakes
The precious landscape of familiar years,
Caress, as women handle silks and furs,
With beams magnetic to give life, awake.

Return, this frozen, heart-enfolded hour,
Rising through shadowed and receding days,
Return with haunting echoes through the cave,
With music's conquering and poignant power.

Return, though vague through veiling years perhaps,
Will still its spell and quickening touch retain,
To ease, relax, smooth out my face again,
To still my breathing, curve and part my lips.

VII

One you might say who walked the clouds of life.
Had known beauty. The snatch of melody
Insistent touched his shoulder, made him pause.
Was widely read. His mind would feel along
To the last tendril, as water in a cave
Fills out each crevice, moulds itself in rock.
Would leave the beaten track. He marked the hawk
Still in its frame of utter loneliness,
Till stone-sheer fall into the pools of green.
White mountains knew his foot-marks, seas his bait.
Friends had been his, giant spirits like himself.
And power of thought explosive to erode
The world of sight and touch, to balance him
Alone on ledge to gaze unflinching on
The central, quiet and enigmatic eye.

All this, but not enough. A hidden beach
Too easy for marauders. Not granite all
His country-side, undaunted to withstand
The glacier's grind and slide, the sea's advance.
Talks on the crops with farmers, chance acquaintances,
With rocket's power in seconds to lift life
Aloft in air and flowering into light,
Life's hedgerows' common growth, all this
Slid off in foam along his iron keel.
A bias from straight course, a gust of wind,
Hand's-breadth deflection, bore him grazing past
The pin-point mark of life, on and away,
To wander aimless through the enormous air.

Sometimes in gaps between his pinnacles,
That flashed in sunlight, made him known far off,
He caught deep down a different instrument,
That played its own tune, obstinate, alone,
Perhaps the sea far off, perhaps a dog,
Lift up its voice and howling at the moon.

VIII

While sleep wells up in oceans as we drive
Past the unruffled river, past the trees'
Long soothing green caress across my eyes,
Your soft words through the landscape of my ease
Heave up smooth inclines, deepening peace, and weave
Into the throbbing twilight of my dreams.
And as you turn to speak to me, your smile
Is gentleness like fading evening light.

PART II

Soldier

ON MY 19TH BIRTHDAY *I left my Devonshire village and began on a different life where writing for a long time had no part. I think I began to feel the compulsion to write again after the Anzio campaign in the summer of 1944. While I was a soldier I wrote one poem only, that entitled Anzio Military Cemetery, where my Winchester friend, who was killed a couple of miles from me and whom I never saw since the day we left Cambridge together, was buried.*

But I had to write and 10 short pieces of prose are included in this book. They are written in pencil on rough pieces of paper, and each has a number, but the numbers are not consecutive, and I meant to write at least 20 pieces. In one sense they express what I wanted to write about. In another sense I see them as evasions. Pick on incidents that are perhaps trivial, and pretend they are what mattered.

The other poems in the second part were written in 1946 when I was back at Cambridge and needed to face the past before I could fully turn my attention to my future. They are not contemporary, but often express my real feelings more completely.

I survived my time in a training unit and was commissioned. After serving for a short time in a regiment in England I was sent on draft via North Africa to Italy, and in November and December 1943 I was in action in the mountains south of Cassino. The first three pieces relate to this time. I was a supernumary officer and had little to do, but a week before Christmas I was sent to take charge of a communications post in a village high on a mountain looking down over enemy country. For the first time I really had a job and related to men of my own. One very young signaller obviously loved me, and so I loved him. The poem is the last of the poems of attraction. The piece of prose shows that the Christmas was special, but makes no reference to the relationship, which was one of attraction, but any question of a sexual element would be suppressed as soon as it arose. Even so when I was a soldier and officer I didn't think it appropriate to mention it.

IX

The line was broken to the Battery Command Post. There was no signaller easily available and another officer was on duty on the troop position, so I went myself to mend it. I walked quickly along the ditch beside the railway bed, running my hand along the wire and climbing over piles of rubble and broken sleepers. My eye was on the wire, and I almost stepped on something before I noticed it. At first it looked like a heap of brown sacking. Then I saw it was a dead man. His leg had been blown off at the knee, and the battledress trousers were still smoking. I looked up and saw that there were half a dozen dead bodies lying in the road. I only noticed that their faces were very pale before I looked away. The line went right under the dead man, and I went on to the exchange for help. I felt slightly sick. They were the first dead men I had ever seen.

X

I have always spent Christmas at home, a Christmas of good food, wine, presents, chocolates, holly, all the usual trappings of an English Christmas. Last year it was different. I spent most of the day coming down from the mountain, which was part of the front line at the time. We had kit to carry on our backs, the country was rough, and I was without a map or any knowledge of the country, and I took a much longer route than was necessary. Yet I will always look back on that Christmas with pleasure. I had been working with these men for some days in bitter weather, cut off in a little world of our own. I think we had grown to like and trust one another. They never complained or lost heart. It was not a normal Christmas, but it was the Christmas of the manger, and in the middle of war it was a Christmas of peace and good will.

XI

Christmas returns. I think of you again,
Whose quiet voice held all my countryside,
Projected on the backcloth of the rain
The look of England like a lantern-slide.
Love's snow-fall softly on my heart descends,
Smooths over harsh upthrusting rocks of pain,
And firelight shuttling through a camera lens
Stamps changing photos of you on my brain.

We did not see Christ born like a dark stranger
With frankincense and gold that chinked and shone,
But rather as shepherds at a humble manger,
Used to the smell of straw we lie upon.
And we, perhaps, as outcasts, born to danger,
Accepted by the suffering Holy One.

Early in January 1944 I was withdrawn to Naples and toward the end of the month I was in action on the Anzio Beachhead. Here I found myself in command of the right-hand troop of guns of the divisional artillery. The other troops had some cover from a line of wood, but mine was exposed, and the Germans had gathered their forces and began to attack expecting to drive us back into the sea. I began by firing four guns with 24 gunners. Five days later I was firing two guns with five gunners and the sergeant major. I have never heard of another artillery troop in Italy that suffered such casualties through shell-fire. I was then sent up to a forward observation post with the infantry, and a few hours later the Germans launched a major attack centred on the battalion I was with, which was overwhelmed. I had to ditch my truck and escape on foot with my three men.

The fourth piece refers to one small incident in this crucial period for my development. The fifth refers to the day following. I watched the enemy lines from the upper floor of the farmhouse which was the battery command post, I think as the only way of giving me something of a rest, as the enemy were too far away for me to see anything significant.

XII

It's queer the thoughts that come to one in the most trying situations. I was at my first Observation Post at Anzio. That evening I decided to deepen the trench I was going to watch from when it became light. I went up with one of my men and a pick and shovel. We set to work. The ground seemed to be solid rock, and each blow of the pick seemed to dislodge no more than a few grains of dust. We were just talking together about whether to give the job us, when without warning the German attack came in. I do not known what their strength was, but they outnumbered us horribly, and it was no discredit to the infantry that they pushed us back. I was right forward and had a very sticky night of it. But every now and then, when things were at their worst, I kept thinking, 'Well any way I won't have to carry on digging that damned slit trench. That's one comfort.'

XIII

It's surprising how many animals you find up in the front line. I was in an Observation Post in the upper story of a house. After a time I looked down to rest my eyes. Below me I saw two oxen. One of them was flat on its side, obviously dead. The other was lying beside it munching a pile of hay. Every now and then it would turn to look at its companion. It seemed to be waiting for it to get up. I had been through quite a tough time those last few days, and I thought I was pretty hardened. But there was something about that sight which went right to my heart, and I said to myself out loud, 'It's a bloody war. It really is a bloody war.'

I survived this period of desperate fighting. My Winchester friend who was an officer in the Scots Guards in the same division did not. The next four pieces need no further explanation.

XIV

I never met you after all.
Our interweaving threads were traced
Across the Mediterranean map,
And still fate cheated us with small
Discrepancies of time and place.
The bullet crossed, and your thread snapped,
Somewhere past Carroceto, where,
Distorted into symbols, farms
Crumble to attitudes of harm,
And death weighs down the air.

And my regret that in my shells'
Saunter or shriek above your head
No word of comfort might be said.
Nor could the bush of smoke unfold
Its insubstantial foliage,
Rising from seeds of iron, to tell
All that my tongue has left untold.
Nor craters on the lettered page
Of pockmarked countrysides indent
Some message to be permanent.

The watchers pace the towers above
The yearning of my starving city,
Their expectation all in vain
For glimpses of your drowning sail.
No more will your excess of love
Within my harbour-wall's embrace
Find haven from unsatisfied
Search of earth for resting place.
My heart for its renewal cries.
O pardon my self-pity.

XV

'Hi, where are you going to? Are you an officer?' It was the Military Policeman outside the town of Anzio who was speaking. I didn't answer him. I was thinking. I thought of the ruined houses round the Flyover Bridge near which I had been the day before at an Observation Post. I thought of the M.P., who had given me cigarettes and an orange, when I went to him for help, dirty and unshaven, because my truck was blocked by a three-tonner slewed across the track, with the driver dead beside it. I thought of Duncan and the others lying very still a few hundred yards from us on the hill. So it had got this far had it? Even on the Beachhead one wasn't safe. The M.P. looked queerly at the strange-looking untidy officer who would not answer him. Didn't he understand English? 'Where are your badges of rank?' he said.

XVI

I went to the Anzio Military Cemetery on an expedition of private grief. Of that I will not write. But this I will say. The graves consist of rows of little rectangles of parched earth, each with a white cross above it. They lie under the high wall of the civilian cemetery with its dark cypresses and shrine. On the other side you look over the rooves of Anzio to the sea. When you in England look at the sea, your minds go out to all the continents and islands spread over the globe, which lie beyond it. It is different for us. Our hearts travel westward, through the Mediterranean, past the Straits of Gibraltar, over the great waves of the Bay of Biscay, to England. Somehow home seems much closer by the sea. I am glad that these men, some of whom I know, lie there. They seem to be buried on the doorstep of their home.

XVII
Anzio Military Cemetery

Outside the civilian cemetery
    With its cypresses and shrines
The pitiful rectangles of dust
    Are dressed in their military lines.

As I search for a name, the crosses
    Grow roots under my feet,
Branching out in innumerable
    Tendrils of private grief.

Death continually weaves his web
    Between the sun and our eyes,
And bars of sorrow shadow the face
    Of others as well as mine.

Silent and tall are the cypresses
    On the other side of the wall.
Perhaps in the depths of their dark hearts
    Hides the reason for it all.

I return through the woods. The sunlight
    Fumbles the top of the trees,
And I feel like searchlights the hostile eyes
    Ceaselessly sweeping the leaves.

And softly the sun goes down in gold,
    And softly the evening falls,
And the stars come out, my comfort,
    But they aren't any comfort at all.

A Field Artillery troop is ordinarily commanded by a captain, whose role is to be at observation posts with the infantry. The second-in-command, a lieutenant, is in charge of the gun position. For the rest of the campaign the gun position did not suffer many casualties, but the troop lost seven officers senior to myself, two of them killed. So for much of the time I combined the roles of both officers and was often at observation posts with the infantry. Numbers XVIII and XIX refer to my next observation post, and XXII and XXIII to later ones. At observation posts one shared the dangers of the infantry, but hand to hand fighting was something I did not experience. The second verse of XXIII suggests that it might be easier than enduring shell and mortar fire. I am sure that for me the verse is quite wrong.

XXV is the last piece on Anzio and the last piece of prose. It shows my passionate commitment to the work I was actually doing and the people and places connected with it. It is true as XVI is questionable. I think I had just about completely forgotten life in England and my home. It may be however that it really was true because it derived from the death of my friend, and he linked Anzio and England in a way that was real to me then.

XVIII

He lifted the tarpaulin for a moment, and I saw him. His head, shoulders and arms were silhouetted black against the canvas. I phoned back fire orders and waited breathlessly for the first round. Our own troops were desperately close and I was afraid it might fall short. There was a whistle, and a cloud of black smoke rose only a hundred yards from the target. A second later came the bang. My third round was almost a direct hit. I put down eight more and had the satisfaction of seeing bits of tarpaulin flying in the air. Then one man ran out of the trench and disappeared over the crest. Five minutes later stretcher bearers approached under a red cross. They removed two bodies and disappeared. For a moment I was triumphant, and then like cold water other thoughts came to me, and I shivered. It was the first time I looked upon men I had killed. A week later I heard that the enemy had dropped a mortar bomb on the trench where I had been and killed two men.

XIX

A small patrol had gone out the night before and had met a strong German outpost. Only one man had got back untouched. That morning I was talking to the Company Commander, when a private shoved his head into the dug-out and asked what he should do with the mail for the dead men. The Company Commander told him to bring them into him. There was a telegram among the letters. He ripped it open and glanced at it, and after a few moments he handed it to me. 'It's from his wife,' he said. I took it from him and read, 'So glad to hear that you are still fit and well.'

XX

Much that is lovely these Italian nights
Red tracers' beautiful parabola.
Hung like a lamp against nocturnal skies
The slow flare burns. Stars veil their eyes before
The angelic visitation, and torn earth
Wavers and stirs under its brilliancy.
And cordite's transient immediate blaze
Leaping like magic genies from the piles
Of sealed green boxes. All these reveal the power
Of fire-works' momentary poignancy.
But are not formed for innocency, are rather
Manifestations of implicit death.
Vainly perhaps the tracer-bullets quench
Their fiery path in earth, or ricochet
Along the rocks. The hands that sped them were
Hungry for human flesh. The flare brings no
Annunciation of a longed for birth.
The golden letters written on sky's wall
Spell rather danger for the working party,

The still grey hummocks dotting no-man's-land.
Far off are watching eyes along the night
Alert to mark the cordite's beacon light,
Success signal, announcement of drawn blood.
Ponderously the gun-barrels swing round
To threatening circles, bode converging death.

XXI

War is not a bit as one imagines. Only once have I felt that I was at war, the war of the cinema and books. I was crossing a mine-field with my major. We were some 300 yards behind our forward positions. Suddenly a flare went up from the German lines. It hung intensely bright in the sky, and we went flat on our faces. I looked round and saw some barbed wire close by, silhouetted against the glare, so clearly that I could make out each spike. Just that, and the two bodies hunched on the ground, and a mortar bomb burst ahead of us as the landscape began to darken.

XXII

I had been in the line with the infantry and was driving back in my jeep to the guns. It was a misty night, and vehicles were hopelessly bogged down all along the narrow muddy track. As we were passing an Advanced Dressing Station an orderly called to us and asked if we would take two infantry-men who had fallen out from the march back to their transport. I managed to squeeze them in, one by the driver and the other at the back with me perched up beside him. He was a nice young fellow and easy to talk to. His voice which was the only physical attribute I could tell was pleasant. The jeep was nosing its way forward sometimes almost sticking in the mud, and twice it nearly overturned. Yet I felt extraordinarily happy and loving to all the world, particularly the infantryman beside me. I had my arm on his shoulder to support myself and the feel was comforting. Yet it was not just he himself personally. He had changed from a normal pleasant acquaintance into a symbol of that body of men whom I honour and admire and pity more than any others, the British infantry.

XXIII

To-night star-grazing mortar bombs
    Drop down the evening sky,
Stamping their signatures, nor care
    Whether we live or die

With hate and human enemies
    Prepared to take our chances.
These monsters, blind, impersonal
    Do not admit of answer.

My limbs take on a private
    And individual life.
Each voice distinct and separate
    Is urgent for relief.

Felt through the veins and arteries
    The whispering blood flows on.
Hard under the flesh the bones
    Mirror the skeleton.

Relayed to dials in the mind
    Each tremor is recorded.
The needle kicks to danger, and
    The warning light glows red.

Carefully lighting cigarettes,
Strangely I hold aloof,
Let time tick on irrelevant,
Nor meet the eye of truth.

Prefer a comprehensible
If incorrect equation,
Rank it with boring visitors,
A long wait at the station.

XXIV

One of the few amenities at Anzio was a bath, a real porcelain bath with a plug. Of course it was in a tent and had no taps, but the attendant filled it with a canvas bucket. It was really a private bath belonging to the Reinforcement Camp, but I always got a good welcome from the attendant when I went down. He had been invalided out of one of the infantry battalions with bad feet, and he liked to talk to some-one who could tell him what was happening up at the front, and a gunner officer knew more than most. Once I did not get down to have a bath for a long time. I eventually managed it, and while the attendant was preparing the bath he looked round and said, 'You know, sir, I thought you'd been killed.' It gave me quite a shock. Then I thought how easily it might be true. It seemed a queer job somehow, to fill baths for people and chat to them, when he quite expected never to see them alive again.

XXV

I heard that the Americans had taken Rome, the final goal of our months of fighting. It didn't excite me much. Rome, Milan, Vienna, Berlin, what were they to me? We had captured what I was interested in, the little villages and farms, and wadis, which I had watched and fired on for so long, places which we had won and lost again and bled for. There were no Germans there now, except dead Germans. Those places are hallowed to me – Carroceto, Pantoni, the Factory, Dead End Road, the Railway Bed, and Buonriposo. Buonriposo in particular. 'After life's fitful fevers they sleep well.'

After we had broken out of the Beachhead and Rome was captured my division was taken out of action. We went into action again in August looking down at Florence. Having shared in the capture of Florence we went up in the Appenines and were finally held up not far from Bologna and the Po valley. In January 1945 we were withdrawn and transferred to Palestine. The war ended and because I was part way through a university course I was demobilised early and was back home in the last few days of that year.

XXVI is the only poem about this campaign, and it is for me the most important of all the poems in this second part. It derives more from my attempts to think through my experiences afterwards than from the experience itself. The poem after it also says something that is important to me.

XXVI

Silence returns. Our gun-flashes no more
Make the horizon dance. Machine-guns cease
Tapping their lunatic morse. Only the breeze
Blows up its whispered memories of peace.

Shadow this hill-top with your hand. Forbid
Shells' shrieked crescendo, burst of seering light.
Keep far the stealthy footsteps of patrols.
My courage drains. Save me at least to-night.

Like giants' fingers, white and fossilised,
Stretch the thin barren ridges from my hill,
Pointing across the dark to those whom we
By mutual contract are compelled to kill.

Save us from hate, and safely guide our feet
Past pit-falls of war's inessential slime.
Only our love can partially redress
These unredeemed and pitiable times.

They through whom widows weep and men become
Bare scaffolding of bones like winter trees,
Somewhere toward the Pole and Cassiopaea
Beyond my range irrelevantly sleep.

Within this valley's amphitheatre stand
Press-ganged the bloody-handed sons of Cain.
Around the white-mantillaed mountains wait
Either with inattention or disdain.

Invisible between us stretch the wires,
The complex net-work of man's common sin.
Relayed each slight electric shock, proclaims
That we are joined by closer bond than kin.

Ceaselessly our owed and guilty blood
Is draining quietly through indifferent ground.
A giant's strength and giant's suffering
Brood a perpetual shadow all around.

The amputation of our gangrened limb
Is necessary evil. May we gain
The surgeon's steady hand and gentleness,
The patient's taut endurance against pain.

XXVII

Retrospect on Fear

The old fears haunt, the downward pull
From tapering unsteady towers,
Watching unhurried streams unwind
Hypnotic spools, that slide behind
A narrow plank. Trapped on the stairs
The night formed solid round my skull.
Or pinned against a swaying bed,
Watching the dull-red foundry glare
Throb slowly in the heart of dark.
Or suddenly on shadowy walls
The pictures writhing into life.

The earth slides open, and the fall
Down sickening shafts, to where a child
Stood in a dungeon paralysed.
And spiders webs spun from the past
Brush on my face and hold me fast.
And then submission, or the climb
Up slimy well-shafts, round my feet
The dragging chains of past defeats.

But when they took and led me bound
And acquiescent to my doom,
I found him in a high white room,
Unshadowed by the undertones
Of all the rising mists of years.
Sat by a window lapped around
By slanting sunlight of relief.
And so I welcomed an unknown
Confined and measurable fear,
And welcoming was borne to peace.

The last poem and much the longest, Victory Day, worries me to read and I am tempted to leave it out, but have not done so. It is the same difficulty that I had in my early poems, trying to write at a depth beyond my experience so that what I write has elements of unreality and falsehood. My way of writing poetry is to use a succession of images. At best these express the truth as I see it, but they can be common-place or derivative. It is necessary for most poets to learn from others, and when I began writing true poetry I naturally read and was moved by the poets of the thirties, Day Lewis, Macneice, Auden and Spender. I was interested in how they wrote poetry, not in any political or social message. The outbreak of war and having to fight had made this aspect of their poetry largely irrelevant, though I had to begin to face such issues after my return. Back at Cambridge I discovered Sidney Keyes, who clearly influenced this poem.

I had to come to terms with the experience of people dying in war, people I was with, people I cared about. I used this poem for that purpose, and I feel I ought to include it. I offer these poems not necessarily because of their profundity or high artistic quality, but as part of a record of what it was like to be one particular person at a particularly significant time.

XXVIII

Victory Day

Read the last bitter page. The book is closed.
Between an end and a beginning Time
Sits a two-headed Janus. Now I call
Impressions from the dark tale of the past,
And the dead come, insistent, drown
All else beneath their over-riding flood,
Chalk-faced and pitiably broken come,
Compelling in their attitudes of death.
All those who died on mountains, whose warm blood
Cut out deep channels, melted tears from snow,
Water and blood, Christ's riven side. Who died
Shattered in hospitals, their minds
Tapered to a white pinnacle of pain.

Those the half-buried in the blowing sand,
Brown heaps of smouldering sacking. Those the green
Extravagant jungle claimed. Those above whom
The wave curled over like a half-closed hand,
Or found an ambush in the innocent air.

You are too many for me. The dark wind
Under whose strong compulsion you are borne
Carries away my words. My bankrupt heart
Cannot contain your numbers. O divide
That I may speak. Let me remember first
All those the great ones, who with open eyes
Walked a straight pathway narrowing up to death.
Taller than us, the strange ground-mists of dawn,
Sidling against them, only on their breasts
Fumbled with ashen fingers, nor could bar
The sunlight's hand in blessing on their brow,
Their still communion with recurring stars.
They stemmed the tide-race, patient like a rock,
Whose roots groped deeper than our fear and pain.
Again they draw our memory. Last seen
Through carriage windows, in the pub at evening,
Dark panelling and amber pints of beer,
Smiled once in the doorway, and went out
Into the black-out, and the door was shut.

Death was a skilful enemy. He knew
Our key positions, vulnerable spots.
All those who never would through pride and love
Step off the pavement so that he might pass,
His equals, these he took.
He was, it seems, particular
About the company he kept.

These were unconquered, died on their own terms.
But what of those the incidentally slain,
Valued for numbers only, whom Death took

Casually in passing on account,
Blank names to swell a casualty list?
These move our hearts. So many they outrun
Memorials or the rivers of our grief.
So many, yet each beyond the price
Of ransoms paid in provinces and gold.
Dazzled their eyes accepted gratefully
Warm darkness like a cloak, and held themselves
Averted from Death's solemn light-house beam
Swinging a golden wheel above their heads.
They planted full-grown forests round their hearts
To hedge them in, their minds held concentrated
A cone of light above their careful hands
Moving in trivial things, till they forgot
The snap of twigs, soft stirring in the leaves.
Or walking as aliens an unreal world
Of wavering shadows and unstable sands,
Dazed by its strangeness, turned and saw far off
A shaft of sunlight striking through the clouds
Pick out the real landscape of the past.

They leave us not the certainty of loss,
The feeling of a million miles of void
Falling around us, but the sense of parting,
Where very absence still affirms their being.
But they are gone, and we who climb a path
Winding into the future from the past,
Bound to our point in time, can never take
A bird's eye view or read the final truth.
The tomb stands dark above us, blotting out
Horizons or the rise of any sun.
Our hearts declare there is no remedy
Against these unhealed wounds. No heir can take
His father's seat, or reinforcement come
To close the gap they left. Where once their touch
Was certain comfort, darkness and the wind.
The vales where corn waved higher, and the birds

Made lovelier music, desert at a step.
We only feel our love grown powerless,
Fretting its heart away inactively,
And pity desperate in the finger-tips
Trembling to reach and help them.

                                              But one word
Of possible comfort in the teeth of death.
They are not dead, but dying. Kneel above
The taut and suffering bodies. Read
The meaning trapped and urgent in their eyes.
The writhing face distorts, and the limbs twitch
In half-formed gestures of the paralysed.
The words fail strangled in constricted throats.
Hard the interpretation, but our debt,
Our duty, and the need for our release
Insistent drive us. For we too have turned
And watched a door swing silently and bar
A way to freedom. Death is not an end.
Rather the wall between adjoining cells.
Muffled the faint and tapped out messages
Still haunt us.

                      Is it this perhaps?
The body dies, the urge for life lives on.
The perishable hands, the earth-stopped tongue,
The doorway closed on their still speaking hearts,
The limbs for movement, these are deeply missed.
And so they hover, where their broken lives
Stand in a chill deserted gallery
Like half-hewn enigmatic statues. Lost
The groped for beauty. Lithe and visioned limbs
Locked in the marble everlastingly.

They plead with us the living. We alone
Have bodies that can satisfy their need,
Unvalued often, yet the only bridge

Between the eternal and the sphere of giving.
They ask our memory, not in the vain laments,
But that their stored up agony of power
May find an outlet through the clasp of souls,
Fan outward from the fountain of the heart,
Drop from our fingers to life-giving earth,
To cheat their death and burst again in flower.
No generous gift they ask us. When we stand
Alone in deserts, all our hope gone dark,
Above our souls spreadeagled on the sand,
Cry out, and they will hear us, come on the wind,
And drive us onward. These our certain aid,
Farther from us than world's end, yet more near
Than enclasped lovers.

                      Now at the point of death
They feel their waters sinking through dark earth
To find their level where the deep-sunk rocks
Are cupped to hold them, there eternally
To wash upon the jagged walls of caves,
To beat like prisoners on the walls of caves.
Channel these waters to your use, to-day
To tend the flowers about remembered shrines,
To-morrow a buried net-work of thin streams,
Threading through subsoil, past the roots of corn,
Sucked down the tendrils' winding passage-ways,
The stems their stairways rising through green towers,
To climb to sunlight and the needed air.

PART III

Return

ALL THE PIECES in the third part are poems and all were written for their own time not as recollections of the past. For me it divides into two sections with XXXIII as the bridge. The early ones link up with the other poems written at that time contained in the second part. I am using poetry to understand and release myself from a past of warfare. Then I am able to move on into my future.

There are no more poems of attraction, but coming to terms with the death of my friend is a compelling necessity. He is the subject of the first and fourth of these poems. The fifth, bridge poem is the last of those about him. It is followed by three poems about religious experience, and it is through the renewing and deepening of my Christian faith that I find reconciliation with the past and capacity to move on into the future.

XXIX

Cambridge Again

The wheel has turned full circle. Now the old
Becomes the new again, and I must cast
About me remnants of a tattered past,
To weave from them fresh garments against cold.

Strange the familiar Gothic silhouettes,
Blunted by memories like mists of tears,
The shadows of the interposing years,
Opaque except to my half-felt regrets.

But sometimes bitterly I find a way
To pick the locks of one time open doors.
Caught in an ambush of the past I pause
Watching my ghost turn down the alley-way,

Glide through the arch-way's sudden slant of gloom,
And casting no intruding shadows where
Low windows spill the moonlight on the stair,
Grope for the handle of your empty room.

Walking this alien court again alone,
The moonlit paving stones beneath my feet
Awake the ancient echoes that repeat,
'For there is nothing old under the sun.'

Most still the water. Almost one might guess
That the reflection was reality.
Not an impossible belief to me
In my inverted and unreal distress.

Above this haunted river can I pray,
My weakness catching at my throat, 'Forget
And cancel my half-paid and bitter debt.
Make my four years ago as yesterday.'

XXX

As you unroll your chess-board
Landscape of black and white,
Old images distress me
Of swans asleep that ride
Still harbours of the past.
Regret that we who know
No unmixed good have lost
The power to make it so.

Your white impersonal surgeons
Drive deep with healing knives,
Carve into shapes most perfect
Our gnarled and twisted lives.
And why should I unmask
The fallible human heart?
Can only ask
For every work of darkness
Your pity and pardon.

XXXI

After the Storm

Changed the squat grizzled buildings,
Their life squeezed out and flattened
By pressure of cloud-ceilings,
    Heavy of head and eye,
A granite Atlas
    Hunched under grey sky.

Now stonework rapt with sunlight,
Floating at their moorings,
As in an antique painting
    Drawn on a gold-washed air,
Angels adoring
    Lift upward eye and prayer.

Reflected in the water
Straight edges are serrated,
Spiral where the leaning
    Willows drowse at peace,
Or concertina
    Suddenly in a breeze.

And water is reflected
On the under-side of arches.
Quick as the eye white patterns
    Like midges weave and dance,
Their vigour contrasted
    With the green water-trance.

Stones like heraldic sun-rays
Fan outward from the open
Mouths of the bridge declaiming
    Quiet words in a grave tongue.
The river is gayer,
    Older but ever young.

To our eyes looking downward
Only the bridge and river,
The dated and the timeless,
    Where past and present cease,
Nor may a frowning
    Future bar our peace.

But may our warm, contracted
Private lives not widen
Again to public danger,
    As grains of sand that pass
Through the dividing
    Neck of an hour-glass.

XXXII

As I stand here so many memories
Come crowding in. Hands trembling on cold gun,
The smell of damp earth as we drive in stakes
    For a new chicken run.

Evenings with fire-dance, lamplight's fairy ring,
The world piled up in lumber in the gloom.
Unseen the hump-backed shadow figures haunt
    Dark corners of the room.

And how familiar landscapes, often an
Unnoticed back-cloth, two-dimensional,
Under our double stereoscopic view
    Were live and actual.

All these are deeply missed, but most of all
The statement of implicit certainties,
The love unearned and unbelievable
    In your confirming eyes.

The last time I looked through them I could see,
Through breaches in words' crumbling barrier-reef,
The dim, unfathomable, sea-green caves
    Ring echoing with grief.

Now only photographs to resurrect
From your impartial, unawakened stare
Something of remembered loveliness, once mine
    Any time and any-where.

XXXIII
All Souls Day

Dust unto dust. The sons of Adam die.
The autumn winds bear unresisting leaves,
And horror's hold grows tight. Your wounds break raw
Over my face. Blood on my lips.
Blood out of bodies. Water into ships.
And earth turns on. O mountainous my grief.

The granite blocks that heavenward I heave
Splinter to rocks I fall on. Outward reach
The blind hands, close on darkness, utter void.
O mine, my lost one, brother of my soul,
Submissive heir, whose wounds succeed
To legacies the spear-struck side bequeathed,
The body broken, making others whole,
Let me go down to find you, let me seek
The veins' tide back to heart, not strive
To force the drag of whirlpools. Walls sweat drops.
Pain's channel narrows, gathers to feet and hours,
And darkness arches over. Poison draws
Down tortured limbs remorselessly, and nerves
Are tattered pennants streaming down the storm
The earth is stilled. Time's moments culminate
To death and birth. Torn hands on trap-door heave.
The body shudders, trembling on light's verge.

Following on the last poem the next three are about religious belief.

XXXIV

My sins have driven up cloud-banks that await
Their cleansing by your mercy and my tears,
And doubts like bats in darkness congregate.
Suppose that we have been, so speak my fears,
    Deceived two thousand years,
    Deceived two thousand years?

We who have known your mercy would be fools
Retracing a hard road to live our time
Standing with pitch-forks above rotting pools,
From which the blind primaeval monsters climb.
    Submerge them back in slime.
    Submerge them back in slime.

Man is not free. Our lives without a pause
Whirl us across the darkness. No release
From the iron rails of your mysterious laws.
Foretold the ancient cycles never cease
    Of sin, repentance and peace,
    Sin and repentance and peace.

The wind is palpable, curbs us as we tack
For disillusioned harbours painfully.
Only if unresisting, wind at our back,
Cutting a white arrow down the sea,
    We find that we are free,
    We find that we are free.

All this we know, though may not understand.
This spar in doubt some safety will afford.
The after-life is hid beneath your hand,
But in your love and service here, O Lord,
    Sufficient our reward,
    Sufficient our reward.

XXXV

Slipping the hawser silently that binds
Us to day's firm and reassuring quay,
Night bears unwilling voyagers to sea
And drifts on an incalculable tide.
Pity for those who with blindfolded eyes
Walk an unsteady plank across the night,
Sheer drop of darkness only left and right,
Not knowing that the sea is quiet and kind.

Those whom the constellations terrify
With old enigmas scrawled across the sky,
Huddled in bed-clothes, senses strained to mark
The certain punctuation of the clock,
The quarters' commas and the hours' full stops,
That nail the sagging curtain of the dark.

XXXVI

To God, unseen, unknown,
The implied final colour, where the faint
Edge of the spectrum fades beyond our sight,
The spirit's journeys, the report of saints,
Walkers in darkness between light and Light,
The intervening darkness where alone
The Light shines and is known.

Here is no place for words,
To turn and summon the distorting light,
Whose lurid fingers will not ever grasp
The hem of the withdrawing robe of night,
But breaks the speaking stillness like a glass,
Vague gestures that disturb
The hover of the snow-white feathered bird.

In mercy, Lord, look down
Upon your clay's presumption and the old
Continual denial by our proof.
Forgive the perishable hands that mould
The sky beneath our rotting timber roof,
The struggles that drag down
The walkers on the water till they drown.

How can your towers be told
By us who skirt the wilderness's fringe,
Striving to smuggle our forbidden loads
Across the frontier's unyielding ring?
Only the trodden and converging roads
Affirm their destination, the unknown
City that calls them home.

The next poem is about renewal of love of the country. My home was now near Huntingdon, and I could not have the same feeling for it as I had for my Devonshire village in very different circumstances.

XXXVII

The sun, the gay town-crier knocks
With something important to proclaim,
Announces a fiesta, slaps
Bright posters on the window-pane.

For Winter muffled slinks away,
A tyrant with his kingdom gone,
And Spring, the new white hope, has got
A good start from the starter's gun.

The trees reopen bankrupt shops,
Their new creations will display.
Gold coins are strewed beneath the hedge.
Squander a fortune in a day.

The birds who carolled yesterday
Held sly rehearsals on their own.
To-day's thanksgiving festival
Will rock the sky's cathedral dome.

The aristocrats will take the air
In austere whiteness on the trees,
Smile at the helter-skelter play
Of bright-clad urchin flowers beneath.

The sun climbs higher, sending out
A challenge as he cries his wares.
And we swear never to repeat
Fiascos of preceding years.

Hard in this densely planted wood
To pick one's own particular tree,
Pin down one aspect, and let slip
The much-desired entirety.

Nor can untwine and isolate
The humming air's ingredients,
Like streamers round a may-pole furled,
Sift through a prism April scents.

The brimstone's indecisive flight
Confuses any coherent trail,
And trees on all sides gaily flap
Their vivid cloaks, distract the gaze.

The fair is in full swing. Green booths
Hide unknown wonders in the wood.
The flowers hold out their trinkets. Bees
Are fortune tellers boding good.

Gilt sunlight, water music lure
To river-eddy's merry-go-round.
Spring drains our purse, who strive to mint
Our moments into pence and pounds.

I had passed beyond the need to write poems of male attraction. My meetings with women had been few and lacking in any real chance to achieve depth. This was now the compulsion upon me. I was anxious and XXXVIII shows something of this anxiety. A friend of mine had an operation, and I visited him at the nursing home. His nurse came in, and I fell in love with her. Her smile linked up with the smile of a boy for whom I had affection at Winchester, and the transition was made. There are two poems about her, one of my first sight of her, and the other of a time when I loved her deeply but thought we would never meet again. In fact we did and we continued our meetings during the period when the poems in this book were being written. The middle verse shows how profoundly memories of war affected my poetry.

XXXVIII
Lady of Night

Come back with the perfumes
    Caught up in your hair,
With music that hovers
    Like birds in the air.
Let fall from your fingers
    The rain-drops of light.
Come back with your loveliness,
    Lady of Night.

The grovelling lamplight
    Bows down at your feet,
Past tenements squinting
    Askew on the street,
Past alleys where nothing
    Has ever gone right.
Come back with your loveliness,
    Lady of Night.

The dogs are all barking
    At cats on the wall.
Come back with your pity,
    Or come not at all.
Come shrouded with horror
    And man-trap delight.
Come back with your loveliness,
    Lady of Night.

XXXIX

Her smile is reminiscent, moves
As life and lantern underground
Through crypt of spirit, shakes a tomb,
And clothes with flesh a skeleton.
Strange resurrection. Memory
Shatters the air with light, and one
With one, alive and dead, are bound
In a dream's double identity

Behind the moment's thin facade
Form the familiar rooms that rise
From palaces sunk underseas.
A present, intimate, alive,
With echoes. Inklings from my past
Fulfil their pattern in rebirth.
Time's lock-gates swinging wide release
Flood-water through an altered earth.

Smashed by a stone-fall is the starred
Ice that reflects illusion, hides
The still form of the wave that slides
From past to future. We diverge
Like river valleys, but our threads
Reach over any ridge that bars,
And, felt this moment, rise to merge,
Gathered in union overhead.

XL

Now she is gone. Paid out the last
Unwilling farthing of the gold
She scattered for me unaware.
Her warmth of being that I cast
Around me like a cloak unfolds,
A net to widen down the air
And drag life from the universe.
Faded her face, and I forget
Her arms like moonlight that have set
With other moons below the earth.

And pain is gone. The ancient wars
Drag on so long that bodies fall
To bury the forgotten cause.
And blood to expiate and bless
Has washed the written papers white
That told the meaning of it all.
And now involuntary hands
Kill almost with gentleness,
And beautiful the dying eyes
Forgive but do not understand.

And I am gone far off, withdrawn
Down lengths of darkened passages,
Infinitely lost and small,
Bowed over on myself to hold
With all my hoarded tenderness
The weight at heart, and to enfold
In a caress of flesh and bone
The dead child never to be born.
And tense the tigress carved in stone
Crouches above with guarding paws.

The next poem puzzles me. What made me write it? But it has much meaning in the light of my life since then.

XLI

More blessed to give, they taught him, than receive.
And so he gave himself, until he found
His trees were dry as matchwood, and his leaves
Hung brittle, dropped and rustled on the ground.
And soon the heels of casual passers-by
Struck tiny fires of malice from the stones,
Though still his warm and automatic smile
Dropped like a safety curtain. But alone
He burned each night his druid sacrifice.
Deep in his heart he scooped a reservoir
To store his rage. Then one day he unfurled
The blood-red banner of a city's fire
Wind-blown and streaming half across the skies,
And turned and laid his curse upon the world.

The last poem is the one that is most important of all of them to me. It sums up the experiences that I had in these years.

XLII

Death's Answer

Love is death's answer only. Hardy bone
Withstands disintegration of the grave.
Admitted through the frontier is alone
A valid coinage to redeem and save.

We are roped on a sheer cliff-face. Felt the stress
Tugging our hearts. When hate's unseen advance
Gnaws through the rocks' foundations, and when death
Knocks out the last stone, brings the avalanche,

May there be something permanent to stand
The slow rot of the weather, and the swing
Across the sawing buttress, while the strands
Sever, unwind, and hang like broken limbs.

Sprouting from hearts our vines of love are splayed
Like river systems branching up the wall.
Make smooth the sap-flow. Let the leaves not fade.
Let shoots grope outward to embrace us all.

And when our hearts are drained, and the stems pin
Us like a new Prometheus on parched earth,
And bones divide like ridges sunken skin,
Grant us your spring's renewal and rebirth.

Temper the links that bind us. Teach
The tension and dependence of the arch,
The spider's blind devotion that may reach
Out with its trailing thread across the dark,

Spun with our agony above the void
The tattered webs inadequately span
Infinities of chaos. O make good
The failure of the love of man for man.

Still underneath are stretched out to sustain
Incalculable the everlasting arms.
Nor bought with your intolerable pain
A body broken and a broken heart.

This windy midnight let your visions rise,
The flesh gleam pallid where the moonlight falls,
And the dark cross be blown aslant the skies.
O God, redeem us all, redeem us all.

Epilogue

ON THE LAST DAY OF 1947 I met a young woman whom I married in the following year. By then I had moved to London to complete my training for the Bar. I wrote one poem to her, but do not include it in this book. Coming to London ended the poetry writing phase of my life. I do not connect it with marriage or my civilian working career. I did not practice at the Bar, but took up other work requiring legal knowledge. I was in one job for the whole of the third quarter of the century. Then I found I needed something wholly different, and involved myself in work for the very poor in London.

One dimension of my need for this change was a desire to return to my youth and something akin to the experience of war that continued to haunt my mind. My comfortable upper middle class home and my first class education had formed a complete contrast with the experience of life in action. In my working life since few have had such contrasts – Buckingham Palace garden parties and a refuge for battered women and children, the official box on the floor of the House of Commons and the House of Lords and Brixton and Holloway prisons, the offices in 10 Downing Street and a shelter for the homeless, Lambeth Palace and a homosexual pad near the Elephant. War when I was young taught me to long for the harmony of conflicting opposites. So in my work since – opposites of male and female, old and young, black and white, rich and poor. But always I have to approach the gap from the side on which I am. I have lived in holes in the ground, I have stood in dole queues at my wits end where to find work, but I have never felt the pressure of desperation for immediate money to keep myself or my family.

In the army there was also the gap, the gap between officer and men, and I had to approach it from my side. Out of action the officers lived together and were privileged. I hated army life out of action. I joined the army because it was necessary to fight. That was what I was there for. In action there was little or nothing in the way of privilege. Having authority could be deeply painful. The main difference between a troop officer who went up to observation posts with the infantry and his gunners was that he was perhaps six times as likely to be killed or wounded. The distinction could add to affection rather than be a barrier against it.

In my writing there is also a gap to bridge. I must stand both by the aging man I am to-day and by the young man I was 50 years ago who still lives within me. This is obvious as far as this book is concerned, but it is also true of everything else I write. When I came up to London and the poetry phase was over I began to write plays. At first they aroused real interest and two were professionally performed, the second even being taken up by a West End company. Then society and the requirements of the theatre changed. It was right that there should be a shift from the dominance of upper and middle class values. Then after I left my main employment I began to write books, autobiographical and fictional. My plays and books were of course written in prose, but always there was a dimension of poetry in them. For both the verdict was the same. 'These are fascinating. We would like to take them, but we cannot see a market for them to-day.'

But I have to stand where I do. I must hold together who I am and who I was 50 years ago as a single whole. It is sad if works of art that follow centuries of tradition and could have communicated a few decades ago should no longer be able to do so. The shift from one set of contemporary values to another is in some ways progress and brings gain, but freeing oneself from influences of the past can involve great loss.

That time 50 years ago was so important to me and still is. Why should it be so? War is horrible in its causes and its operation, horrible and insane. But the individual human being lives in his own situation.

At that time I was conscripted to love. I was placed in a situation where I was willing as a matter of course to lay down my life for my friends. Love goes beyond power, beyond wisdom. Love goes outward beyond any limits.

'O God, redeem us all, redeem us all.'